TELL ME WHY, TELL ME HOW

WHY DOES IT THUNDER AND LIGHTNING?

DARICE BAILER

 **Marshall Cavendish**
Benchmark
New York

Special thanks to Dr. Don MacGorman, a physicist at the NOAA/National Severe Storms Laboratory in Norman, Oklahoma, for his consultation in helping explain the latest theories of thunder and lightning to children.

Other Marshall Cavendish Offices:
Marshall Cavendish International (Asia) Private Limited, 1 New Industrial Road, Singapore 536196 • Marshall Cavendish International (Thailand) Co Ltd. 253 Asoke, 12th Flr, Sukhumvit 21 Road, Klongtoey Nua, Wattana, Bangkok 10110, Thailand • Marshall Cavendish (Malaysia) Sdn Bhd, Times Subang, Lot 46, Subang Hi-Tech Industrial Park, Batu Tiga, 40000 Shah Alam, Selangor Darul Ehsan, Malaysia

Marshall Cavendish is a trademark of Times Publishing Limited

All websites were available and accurate when this book was sent to press.

Library of Congress Cataloging-in-Publication Data
Bailer, Darice.
  Why does it thunder and lightning? / by Darice Bailer.
     p. cm. — (Tell me why, tell me how)
  Includes index.
  Summary: "Provides comprehensive information on the process of thunder and lightning happening"—Provided by publisher.
  ISBN 978-0-7614-4825-9
  1. Thunderstorms—Juvenile literature. 2. Lightning—Juvenile literature. I. Title.
  QC968.2.B35 2011
  551.55'4—dc22
  2009033495

Photo Research by Candlepants Incorporated

Cover Photo: Paul Avis / Getty Images

The photographs in this book are used by permission and through the courtesy of:
Getty Images: Photography by Steve Kelley aka "mudpig" , 1; Dennis Hallinan, 4, 13; Lyle Leduc, 5; Steve Allen , 8; Michael Hirsch, 9; Samuel D. Barricklow, 15; Ryan McVay, 16; Harald Sund, 20; Gandee Vasan , 21; Phil Schermeister, 22; Erik Simonsen, 23. *Art Resource, NY*: Erich Lessing, 6. *Photo Researchers Inc.*: Sheila Terry, 7; Roger Harris, 12; Gary Hincks, 14. *Alamy Images*: B.A.E. Inc., 10; Scott Camazine, 11. *Corbis*: Martyn Goddard, 17. *Marshall Cavendish Image Library*: 19.

Editor: Joy Bean
Publisher: Michelle Bisson
Art Director: Anahid Hamparian
Series Designer: Alex Ferrari

Printed in Malaysia (T)

1 3 5 6 4 2

CONTENTS

It is fun to play outside with your friends in the rain. But if you hear the sound of thunder, you should all go inside as quickly as you can.

What is a Thunderstorm?

On a dark gray day, you might see a flash of lightning. A bright light flickers in the sky and then BOOM! You hear thunder. The air cools and rain starts to fall. You feel it on your nose and the top of your head.

Thunderstorms light up dark skies like fireworks. A thunderstorm has claps of thunder and lightning, and it can last just a few minutes or many hours.

Lightning can sometimes light up the whole sky so you can see for miles.

Every day, there are about 44,000 thunderstorms around the world. Altogether these thunderstorms produce about fifty flashes every second. Scientists estimate that lightning strikes the earth about one million times a day!

How lightning works was a mystery for a very long time. Long ago, people thought angry gods threw lightning bolts down from the sky. Ancient Greeks believed that Zeus, the father of the gods, hurled thunderbolts to punish people. Africans believed that a giant bird-god beat his great wings in the sky to make thunder. Native Americans called this bird a "thunderbird" and thought that it shot lightning out of its eyes.

Benjamin Franklin was a famous American and one of

This painting shows Zeus holding lightning bolts. In ancient times, people did not know where lightning came from so they made up the story of Zeus to explain why lightning happened.

the fathers of our country. A scientist, Franklin thought he knew what caused lightning. And, one day in 1752, Benjamin ran outside to test his idea. The sky was dark

Benjamin Franklin tried to learn what caused lightning by experimenting with a kite and a key.

with storm clouds as he gathered up a kite. He tied a key to the bottom of a kite string. He also tied a silk ribbon to the end of the kite string and wrapped it around his fingers. Thunder cracked and it was dangerous for Franklin to be outside. But he wanted to fly his kite to see if he was right.

What did Franklin want to prove? And, why does it thunder and lightning? Keep reading to find out.

This cumulonimbus cloud means that rain, thunder and lightning are likely on the way

What Makes Thunderstorm Clouds?

A tall, dark thundercloud is called a **cumulonimbus cloud**. In Latin, *cumulus* means "heap" and *nimbus* means "rain". But how do rain and clouds form?

On a warm day, the sun shines and heats the ground. This dries up water on the grass, sidewalk, and other surfaces. All this water escapes into the air. When the water on these surfaces escapes into the air, it is evaporating, or becoming a gas called **water vapor**.

Water can be a liquid, solid, or gas and it can change from one form to the other. The water you drink is a

The process of rain starts through evaporation. When the sun warms up the air around this grass, the water on it will begin to evaporate.

liquid. But if you pour water into a tray and freeze it, that liquid will turn into a solid—ice. And, if you boil water, you can see it steam up and turn into water vapor. Because water vapor is a gas, it gets mixed in with the rest of the air nearby.

If some of the air is a little warmer than the air around it, that air is lighter, too, and so rises. As warm air travels up into the sky, it cools. The farther you travel away from the surface of the earth, the colder it gets. And, when the rising air cools enough, the water vapor mixed up in the air **condenses** and becomes a liquid again. The water vapor turns from a gas back into very small drops of water. Billions of tiny water drops form a cloud.

High up in the **atmosphere**, it is cold enough for water to

One of the easiest ways to see evaporation in action is watching water in a tea pot boil. The steam you see is water vapor.

10

freeze. Tiny droplets of water freeze into ice crystals. These heavier crystals fall through the cloud and crash into more water droplets. When they do, the drops of water freeze onto the ice crystals, making the ice bigger and forming soft hail. This soft hail helps create electrical forces that cause lightning!

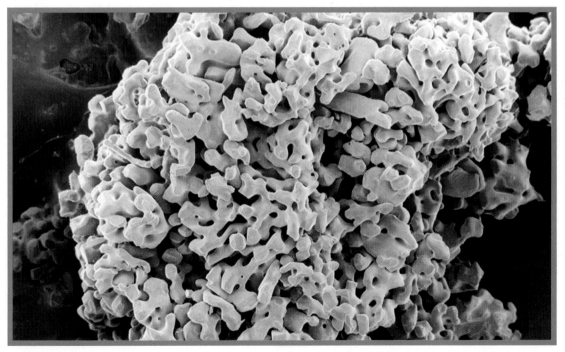

This photograph shows soft hail, as seen through a microscope. Soft hail helps trigger lightning.

This computer illustration shows the structure of an atom. Electrons are in blue, neutrons are in green, and protons are in red. Protons and neutrons make up the **nucleus** (center) of the atom. Electrons move around the nucleus.

How Does a Thunderstorm Begin?

Ice crystals and droplets and everything else in the world are made of pieces that are so small you cannot see them. These **invisible** pieces are called **atoms**.

Air, water, and even your own body are made of atoms. Atoms are so small that millions could fit on the eraser of your pencil. Yet each atom is made up of even smaller parts called **protons**, **electrons**, and **neutrons**.

Protons and electrons have something called **electric charge**. Charges are positive or negative, and charges that move make an **electric current**. Electric currents make **electricity** so that

Everything in this photo is made is made up of atoms—the rain, the umbrella, and even the child's skin and hair.

machines, televisions, and light bulbs can work. Electric currents get lightning going as well.

When wind whips upward through a tall cloud, small hail collides with tinier pieces of ice inside a storm cloud. And, as they bump into each other, some pieces of ice lose electrons and some pieces of ice gain electrons. When this happens, they exchange electrical charges. The exchange of charges can create a very strong electric force. The force can be strong enough to cause lightning.

Down on the ground, all we see is the bottom of the dark storm clouds. The water and ice in a tall thunderstorm

Positive and negative charges are attracted to each other. In a thunderstorm, some of the lightning that begins in the cloud keeps moving toward the positive charge in the ground.

act a bit like a bunch of tiny mirrors. They reflect much of the sunlight toward the top and sides of the cloud. That makes the top and sides of clouds appear bright white. But it keeps much of the sunlight from reaching the bottom of a storm cloud. This makes the bottom of the cloud look dark and gray. Those dark clouds mean a thunderstorm is coming.

Thunderheads are the towering clouds you see during thunderstorms. A single thunderhead can cause a storm with lightning.

When you drag your feet across a rug, such as the one in this photo, you are picking up lots of electrons.

When Lightning Strikes

Have you ever dragged your shoes across a rug during the winter? When you do this, you are picking up electrons! The rubbing action makes the electrons stream up from the rug and onto the soles of your shoes. The rug loses electrons and you gain them. Electrons flow up your legs, through your body, and down to your fingers.

The electrons make your fingers have a **negative charge**. And if you reach for a metal doorknob with your fingers, you will soon find out that the negative charge on your fingers makes the metal doorknob have a **positive charge**.

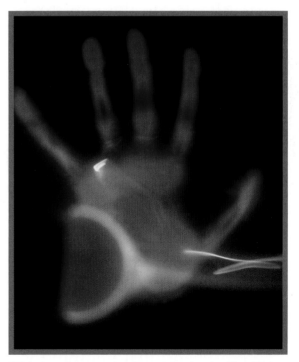

This is what static electricity looks like. This is the moment of the spark you feel and sometimes see.

17

Positive charges attract negative charges and negative charges attract positive charges. When your negatively charged fingers get closer to the positively charged doorknob, the **electric force** between the two increases. When your finger gets close enough, then—zap! You create a tiny **spark** and feel a shock!

Something like that happens inside the dark storm cloud. Wind stirs up the rain, hail, and ice crystals. The heavier hail falls and collides with the smaller ice crystals and the two exchange charge. As more and more soft hail forms and falls, the amount of charge increases and the electric force builds.

The electrically charged cloud makes the earth have a positive charge, the same way the negative charge on your finger makes a doorknob have a positive charge. A giant spark jumps through the air, and it looks like lightning is just coming out of the bottom of a cloud. But electric sparks also skyrocket up from the ground and the sparks meet and connect. Together they make one giant spark—lightning! A whole lightning flash usually lasts less than one second.

Benjamin Franklin thought that thunderstorms contain charge and that lightning is a form of electricity. When he took his key on a kite string out in that storm in 1752, he proved that his thought was correct. The charge in the clouds above him made an electric current flow through the kite string to the key.

This illustration shows lightning striking a building. The large amount of negative charge in the cloud makes most of the earth beneath the cloud have a positive charge. The attraction grows between the cloud and the ground, and a spark jumps down from the cloud (image 2) and then up from the building (image 3). When the two sparks meet, they make one giant spark called lightning (image 4).

Lightning follows a crooked path through the air. Most lightning that you see is at lea 5 miles (8 kilometers) long.

What Causes Thunder?

One of the scariest things about thunderstorms is the sound of thunder. Thunder is one of the loudest sounds in the world. And, the closer the lightning is to you, the louder the thunder sounds.

A flash of lightning can be very, very hot—greater than 50,000 degrees Fahrenheit (28,000 degrees Celsius). The surface of the sun is only 11,000 °F (6,093 °C), which means lightning is almost five times hotter! A single flash of lightning is brighter than 10 million light bulbs. It lights up the entire sky!

Lightning usually strikes the tallest object in its path because it is the easiest path for the lightning to take.

But then you blink your eyes, and the lightning is gone. The electric current that flows through the sky heats the air so fast that the air explodes. The explosion causes a rumbling or a loud BOOM in the sky.

The light and thunder from lightning start moving toward us at the same time. But light moves nearly a million times faster than sound. Since light travels faster than sound, we see lightning first. Then we hear thunder.

When lightning strikes over 12 miles (19 km) away, such as out in the ocean, it is usually too far away to hear thunder.

If lightning strikes the ground close to you, the thunder you hear sounds like a loud bang. When lightning is a little farther away it makes thunder sounds like loud claps. When it is even further away the thunder sounds like rumbling. And if lightning strikes more than 12 miles (19 kilometers) away, it is usually too far to hear any thunder.

Lightning is dangerous because a very large electric current flows through it.

Now I Know!

What is thunder?

It is the sound of lightning. Lightning heats up the air so quickly that the air explodes.

Whenever you hear thunder, quickly go inside your house or another building. If lightning strikes you, it can be deadly.

Not all lightning strikes the ground. Most lightning stays inside the clouds. Sometimes lightning leaps from one cloud to another. There is even lightning that shoots far out the top or side of a cloud.

Thunderstorms can bring heavy rain, hail, and flash floods. Their lightning can cause forest fires. Thunderstorms can be very helpful as well. They bring rain to nourish plants and soil and to refill our rivers and oceans. And, we are still learning more about them.

 Activity

You can hear a smaller version of thunder anytime you want in your own home. All you need is a balloon and a woolen blanket, rug, or sweater—and a very quiet room! Blow up the balloon, rub it back and forth over the woolen object for about thirty seconds, and listen carefully. Do you hear the little crackling sound of tiny sparks between the balloon and the wool? Sparks make that sound in the same way that lightning makes thunder!

This activity does not work as well on humid days when the air has a lot of water vapor in it. It works best on days when the air is very dry.

When you rub the wool against the balloon, you are like the wind causing soft hail and ice crystals to bump against each other in a storm cloud. You are helping electrons move. Electrons can move from one piece of ice to another when the pieces of ice collide inside a storm cloud, and they can leap from the sweater to the balloon when you rub the sweater and balloon together.

When sparks flow through the air between positive and negative charge during a thunderstorm, the electric current is so hot that the air explodes. When you rub the balloon over the wool, they do not touch in some places, but are very close together. In places where they are close but not touching, very small sparks can flow through the air to carry some of the electrons that the balloon has captured back toward the sweater. The electric current that flows in the small sparks also heats the air and creates a small crackling sound. This crackle is a little like the loud thunder you hear during a thunderstorm from the giant spark of lightning.

It takes thunder about five seconds to travel one mile. So the next time you see lightning in the sky, start counting the seconds. Then stop counting when you hear the clap of thunder. Next, divide that number by five. The answer will tell you how many miles away the lightning is. For example, if you count to ten, lightning is two miles away. Sometimes you cannot hear the thunder because the lightning is too far away or the wind is too strong.

1) What happens if you count to twenty? How many miles away is the storm?

2) What happens if you count to thirty? How many miles away is the storm?

3) How far away is the storm if you count to thirty-five?

Glossary

atmosphere—The air.

atom—The tiny building blocks that make up everything in the universe.

condense—To change a gas, or water vapor, into liquid.

cumulonimbus cloud—A tall, dark cloud that is often a sign of a thunderstorm. These clouds are also called thunderheads.

electric charge—Every atom is made up of protons, electrons and neutrons. In the middle of the atom is a nucleus which contains the protons and neutrons. Electrons orbit around the nucleus. Protons have a positive charge and electrons have a negative charge. Positive charges are attracted to negative charges and negative charges are attracted to positive charges. Charge is what keeps electrons orbiting around the nucleus.

electric current—The flow of electric charges from one place to another. *Current* means "running" or "flowing".

electric force—An invisible attraction between positive and negative electric charges. This force draws a negatively charged electron toward a positively charged particle.

electricity—The movement of electrons or electric currents to create one kind of energy.

electrons—The parts of an atom that move around the center of an atom and have a negative charge of electrical energy.

invisible—Something that cannot be seen.

negative charge—An atom with extra electrons. When atoms gain electrons, they are negatively charged.

neutrons—The parts inside the nucleus of an atom that have no electric charge.

nucleus—The center of an atom which is made up of protons and neutrons.

positive charge—An atom that is missing electrons. When atoms lose electrons, they have a positive charge.

protons—The positively charged parts of an atom.

spark—A flash of light made when electrons move suddenly through the air in a thin electric current. This electric current heats the air and makes it shine.

water vapor—The gas produced when water evaporates.

 Find Out More

BOOKS

Hamilton, John. *Lightning*. Edina, MN: ABDO Publishing Company, 2006.

Hidalgo, Maria. *Lightning*. Mankato, MN: Creative Education, 2007.

Mayer, Cassie. *Thunder and Lightning*. Chicago: Heinemann Library, 2007.

McTavish, Douglas. *Fried! When Lightning Strikes*. London: A & C Black Publishers Ltd., 2009.

Simon, Seymour. *Lightning*. New York: Collins, 2006.

WEBSITES

A movie that shows how clouds and lighting form and how to be safe during a thunderstorm.
www.kidsknowit.com/interactive-educational-movies/
    free-online-movies.php?movie=Lightning

Cool facts about lightning along with pictures, safety tips and experiments
www.weatherwizkids.com/weather-lightning.htm

Facts and activities about weather from the National Oceanic and Atmospheric Administration
www.education.noaa.gov/sweather.html

 # Index

Page numbers in **boldface** are illustrations.